The Catcher
in the Rye:
A Reader's Guide to the
J.D. Salinger Novel

ROBERT CRAYOLA

CONTENTS

INTRODUCTION

Welcome to *The Catcher in the Rye: A Reader's Guide to the J.D. Salinger Novel.* This guide will add to your understanding of the book and get you thinking about its deeper dimensions. We will examine it from a variety of angles and this will be beneficial whether you are totally new to the book or have already familiarized yourself with the text.

The Catcher in the Rye has been a bestseller for over sixty years now. Something about it has touched a chord with readers, especially young people. We'll try to find out what its appeal is in this guide.

Let's begin our study by looking at the author, J.D. Salinger.

AUTHOR: Jerome David Salinger was

born in New York City on January 1, 1919. He was raised Jewish but would later learn that his mother wasn't actually Jewish. He published in school newspapers growing up and was socially active in numerous clubs.

After high school, he began college at NYU but soon dropped out. He tried to make it in the meat-packing industry, even going to Austria for the business, but he quickly returned just before the Nazis annexed Austria.

He began college once more in Pennsylvania and again dropped out. He continued writing, however, and took a writing class at Columbia University. He had his first story professionally published in *Story* magazine in 1940. He would submit stories to the *New Yorker* and finally had "Slight Rebellion off Madison" accepted, but because of the war references, it was not published until 1946. It featured the character of Holden Caulfield, later the narrator in *The Catcher in the Rye*.

In 1942 Salinger was drafted and served active duty during several major battles. While in Europe, he arranged to meet Ernest Hemingway, whom he respected. Hemingway saw great promise in the young writer and encouraged him.

Salinger continued to write and submit stories during the war, but he suffered a great deal of traumatic stress. When the war ended, he married a German woman and returned with her to the U.S. The marriage failed after eight months and she returned to Germany.

Salinger tried to have a book of stories published at this time, but the deal fell through. He continued to write and publish, and with the publication in The New Yorker of "A Perfect Day for Bananafish" he secured a contract with the magazine that gave them first-rights to publish his stories. He would release short works mainly through them for the remainder of his career. The story would mark the first appearance of the Glass family, and Salinger would use them in numerous other stories.

About this time, he also took a strong interest in Zen Buddhism. It would be the first of many schools of thought to interest him. He would take his practices very seriously and often encourage or force others close to him to adhere to his systems.

In an attempt to secure more money, Salinger sold the film rights of a story to Hollywood and they turned it into *My Foolish Heart*. He hated the film and vowed to never have one of his works mutilated in that way again.

In the late 40s Salinger began work on his first novel, *The Catcher in the Rye*. It featured Holden Caulfield from his earlier story and was a semi-autobiographical tale of a disaffected youth. It would be published in 1951 to enormous success, earning critical acclaim, banned in some countries and schools, and still selling about 250,000 copies a year to this day.

A second book followed in 1955: *Nine Stories*, collecting a variety of material. It was also successful. Salinger's growing fame was unwelcome, and he moved from New York to New Hampshire and began to live a more reclusive lifestyle, also publishing less. He married in 1955 and had two children before divorcing in 1967. He would publish his two final books in the early 1960s: *Franny and Zooey*, and *Raise High the Roof Beam, Carpenters and Seymour: An Introduction*. His final published work was a novella in 1965.

Salinger's home life is reported as being regimented and peculiar. It's hard to say how accurate these descriptions are. They mainly come from writer Joyce Maynard, who had a 9-month relationship with Salinger in 1972 when she was 18 and he was 53, and his daughter Margaret Salinger. Scrutiny in the reclusive author didn't abate. His son would denounce the viewpoint told by Salinger's daughter in her memoir, leaving many questions unanswered. Salinger died on January 27, 2010 at age 91, and scrutiny and interest by fans continue to this day with the release of the documentary *Salinger*.

CONTEXT: We should keep the book's era in mind when we read it. It seems to take place in the late 1940s when America was beginning to experience a new prosperity. People had returned from World War II and wanted a safe family life, the American dream of a home, and steady work. Much of this will be lambasted in Holden Caulfield's narration. He can't stand the mindless conformity and stupidity he sees all around him. In a sense, his feelings will erupt in the 1960s, but he is a little too early, and he would probably find the 60s as easy to criticize as any era.

THE ELEMENTS OF LITERATURE

WHAT KIND OF BOOK IS THIS?: *The Catcher in the Rye* is an average-length *novel*.

STRUCTURE: The book is divided into 26 chapters. 25 chapters are devoted to Holden's narration of events over a few days before Christmas. The last short chapter has Holden reflect on his story.

SETTING: Setting is the time and place that a story occurs. The time is the late 1940s. The book begins with Holden at a private high school in the fictional town of Agerstown, Pennsylvania. He will leave there after a few chapters and the remainder will take place in New York City.

NARRATOR AND P.O.V.: The narrator

is Holden Caulfield, one of the most famous characters in fiction. His is 16 years old for the events in the novel. He is very disgruntled about almost everything and doesn't know what to do with himself. We might question the accuracy of much of his story. When a narrator cannot always be trusted to be 100% accurate, we call him or her an *unreliable narrator*. Although we can trust the general accuracy of events, Holden might not always relate the details completely right, softening things to make him look better and others look worse.

TENSE: The book is "written" by Holden a few months after the story's events and is written in the past tense.

TONE: Tone is how a book *feels*. Because Holden is bitter about many things in the book, the tone is very pessimistic. Rarely a page passes without Holden describing something as depressing.

PLOT: The story of *The Catcher in the Rye* concerns Holden Caulfield and how he spends a couple of days before Christmas. He is a teenager attending a private school in Pennsylvania, and he is kicked out. It is the latest in a series of schools to kick him out for underperformance. Rather than remain a few more days at the school, he decides to leave for New York (where his family lives) early and stay in a cheap hotel.

Over the next few days he has a series of encounters with various people in all walks of life. His overall attitude is one of pessimism and depression, and the adventures he has only serve to make him feel worse. He almost loses his virginity to a prostitute, gets beat up by her pimp, goes to various bars trying to get drunk, and meets a few old friends.

When his money runs out he sneaks into his parents' home and borrows more cash from his younger sister Phoebe. He decides he will hitchhike out west and start a new life for himself. However, when he meets his sister again to return her money, she convinces him not to run away. The book concludes with Holden recovering from a nervous breakdown in California, reflecting on the experience of those few days.

PROTAGONIST: The protagonist is the main character or person we have most sympathy with. In this book that is the narrator, Holden Caulfield.

ANTAGONIST: The antagonist is what opposes the narrator, often in the form of a person or people. There isn't *one* antagonist in the book – instead, Holden faces *many* people who are part of a society of "phonies," as he views them, people who are not genuine with their feelings and behavior.

CONFLICT: Conflict is the struggle a character goes through. Holden's conflict is a struggle to live an authentic life and not be crushed by the mindless conformity he sees all around him.

CLIMAX: The climax is the moment of greatest tension in the story, the point when a character will not be the same again. It comes for Holden when he is preparing to abandon his family and life in the city and try to hitchhike out west and start a new life. It seems like he might do it, but he succumbs to the wishes of his sister instead.

RESOLUTION: The resolution is how the story unwinds after the climax has passed. Holden tells us he will stay in the city after all. He accedes to the wishes of his family. We jump ahead a few months to see him recuperating out west. We don't know exactly what his future will be like, but he seems to have recovered his balance a little.

BOOK TITLE: The title comes from Holden's misremembering of an old folk song called "Comin' Thro' the Rye," popularly published by poet Robert Burns. He imagines children playing in a field of rye near the edge of a cliff, and a "catcher" who would stand near the edge of the cliff and make sure children don't go over the edge. When Holden's sister Phoebe asks him what he'd like to be, he tells her "a catcher in the rye."

THEMES: Themes are what the author chooses to highlight through the use of story. Some of the themes in *The Catcher in the Rye* include:

The inauthentic quality of the world (especially the adult world of "phonies")

The feelings of being an outsider

How we put on different masks for different people and situations

The weight of responsibility placed on us

CHARACTERS

HOLDEN CAULFIED – Holden is the narrator and protagonist of the book. He is sixteen years old for most of the story, over six feet tall, and thin. He is a depressed and cynical person who dislikes a great deal of the world. We'll follow him over a few days as he leaves his private school and explores different parts of the city and tries to find a real connection to people.

D.B. CAULFIELD – D.B. is Holden's older brother. He works and lives in Hollywood as a writer. Holden thinks he has sold out to Hollywood. When Holden is recuperating in California at the end of the book, D.B. will visit him.

HOLDEN'S PARENTS – Holden's

parents aren't shown directly interacting with Holden. We know his father is a corporate lawyer who makes a great deal of money. Holden worries about their reaction when they'll hear that he was kicked out of another school. They return from a party when Holden sneaks into their apartment later in the book.

PHOEBE CAULFIELD – Phoebe is Holden's younger sister and the person he connects most closely with. She is smart, opinionated, and good at reading through Holden's lies. Her anger with Holden keeps him from hitchhiking out west.

ALLIE – Allie is Holden's dead younger brother. Allie died of leukemia when he was only 11. Holden prays to him when he feels depressed or scared.

MR. SPENCER – Before Holden leaves the Pencey Prep school to return to New York, he goes to speak with his history teacher Mr. Spencer. He is an old man who lectures Holden. He reads Holden's essay test answer to him. Holden wishes he hadn't come to see him.

WARD STRADLATER – Stradlater is Holden's roommate at Pencey Prep. He is big, conceited, handsome, and rich. Holden calls him a moron repeatedly and Stradlater punches him in the face.

ROBERT ACKLEY – Ackley is in the neighboring room of Holden at Pencey Prep. He is an 18-year-old senior, very tall, has bad teeth, and poor social skills. Holden doesn't really like him, but he goes to see Ackley after being punched in the face by Stradlater.

MAL BROSSARD – Brossard is a friend of Holden's at Pencey Prep. He goes with Holden and Ackley downtown on a snowy day before Holden leaves the school.

SALLY HAYES – Sally is a girl Holden has dated. He calls her up when he returns to New York and has a date with her. He imagines going away with her and enjoying a quiet life in the woods. Later, she'll get on his nerves and he'll hurt her feelings.

JANE GALLAGHER – Holden knew Jane before the events of the novel and he wants to get in touch with her, but he never does during the course of the book. Stradlater had a date with her and Holden worries how far she went with him. He views Jane with a sense of nostalgia and esteems her higher than most characters in the book.

MRS. MORROW – Mrs. Morrow is the mother of a student Holden knows at Pencey Prep. He meets her on the train to New York and finds her very nice and attractive. He tells her all kinds of lies about himself and her son Ernest.

FAITH CAVENDISH – Faith is a woman Holden phones when he arrives in New York and tries to meet for a drink. He obtained her number from another boy he knew, and Faith is reputed to have a reputation for looseness. She is unable to meet him, however.

ERNIE – A pretentious piano player Holden goes to see at a club he used to frequent with his brother D.B.

MAURICE – An elevator operator who convinces Holden to take a prostitute. They agree on five dollars as the charge, but the girl he sends says the price is ten. Maurice comes to Holden's room and roughs him up to get the money.

SUNNY – The prostitute Maurice sends to Holden's room. She is young and irritates Holden. He decides he can't go through with having sex with her. She returns with Maurice to collect five more dollars from Holden.

LILLIAN SIMMONS – Lillian is an old girlfriend of Holden's brother D.B. that he runs into at Ernie's club. She is with a navy guy and Holden excuses himself to get away from her.

CARL LUCE - Carl is a student Holden

knew from a previous school. He is an older boy and seems sophisticated to Holden. They meet for a drink and Holden asks him persistent questions about his sex life.

MR. ANTOLINI – Antolini is a former teacher of Holden's who has maintained contact with the Caulfield family. He is a young man and married to an older woman. He allows Holden to sleep on his couch. He lectures Holden and then disturbs him very much by petting or patting his head as he sleeps. Holden isn't sure if Antolini is making a pass at him.

CHAPTER SUMMARIES & COMMENTARY

CHAPTER 1: The book begins with a somewhat unusual narrator: Holden Caulfield. He tells us right away that he doesn't want to go into the full details of his life, "all that David Copperfield kind of crap," as he puts it, referring to the Charles Dickens character. He tells us that he's only going to talk about the "madman stuff that happened to me around last Christmas." We won't find out what he means by madman until later. But essentially Holden is kicked out of his private high school and has a nervous breakdown by the end of the book. He's narrating the story from out in California, where he seems to be at some kind of sanitarium to relax and restore his mental health.

But the book begins in Agerstown, Pennsylvania, where Holden attends a private school called Pencey Prep. It's a Saturday just before Christmas, and there is a big football game that everybody is at. We see in Holden's descriptions that he complains about almost everything. He's a bitter, angry young man about most of the world, and that's part of why a lot of young people have latched onto the book so strongly – they see in Holden's attitude something they can really relate to.

Holden says that he just got back from New York with the fencing team and that he's going to speak with Mr. Spencer, his history teacher, who requested Holden see him before he left. He arrives at the house and see that Mr. and Mrs. Spencer are very old. She is a little hard of hearing, and sends Holden in to speak with Mr. Spencer.

CHAPTER 2: Holden goes into the house and speaks with Mr. Spencer, his history teacher, and he's immediately depressed and regrets the visit. Becoming immediately "depressed" by something he sees or hears is a common occurrence for Holden and we'll see it happen many times in the book. Concerning Mr. Spencer, Holden is depressed by the man's old age and decrepit state, plus the lecture he gives Holden.

We learn some more about Holden. He says he's about 6' 2.5" tall, 16 years old at the time of the story, and that he's been kicked out or quit several other schools. The general reason seems to be that Holden doesn't apply himself to his work. He doesn't care about school, and that he's not too worried about his future because his family is pretty well off.

Mr. Spencer reads some of Holden's weak essay to him, and that really turns Holden against the old man. He calls it a "dirty trick" to do that to him. He cautions Holden some more about his future, and then Holden tells him he has to leave to go to the gym. He thinks Mr. Spencer yells "Good luck!" to him as he leaves, and Holden really doesn't like this.

We see in this chapter that Holden vacillates between emotions quickly. He's defensive and easy to offend, and he retreats when things don't go how he wants them to. He also describes many people in the book as "phonies" – he is searching for more authenticity in life and not finding it. On the other hand, we're going to see Holden put on several different "fronts" throughout the book, showing that he can be phony in his own way as well. He often has a double standard for himself and the world.

CHAPTER 3: Holden tells us that he's a terrific liar (and we'll see that in the book), because he doesn't actually have to go to the gym. He just said that to get away from Mr. Spencer. Instead, he goes back to his dorm room. He lives in a wing of the building named after a man named Ossenburger, who made his fortune in undertaking. Holden says he came to speak at their school and a boy farted loudly during his speech. Holden found it amusing because he thinks Ossenburger was full of himself.

Holden gets back to his room that he shares with a boy named Stradlater, who is gone. Most of the dorm is empty because everyone's at the football game. Holden starts rereading Isak Dinesen's *Out of Africa* and says he likes a book that makes you want to chat with the author. He is interrupted in his reading when Robert Ackley, a boy in the neighboring room, pokes his nose in. Ackley is described by Holden as tall and having unclean teeth. He tries to make it clear to Ackley he wants to be left alone, but Ackley won't leave. Finally, Holden puts his book down and starts fooling around, acting blind underneath the red hat he bought in New York that day. They talk a few minutes more, generally complaining about things and each other, until Holden's roommate Stradlater comes in. Ackley doesn't like Stadlater and leaves. Stradlater asks to borrow Holden's jacket, and goes for a shave.

This is the first time we've seen Holden interact with his peers. They behave somewhat like typical teenage boys, but Holden seems to have an underlying recognition that he's leaving soon and will probably never see these boys again. Even though he dislikes a lot about each of them, he's capable of recognizing some good things about them. But like before, he will vacillate between emotions and easily be provoked to annoyance.

CHAPTER 4: Bored, Holden talks with Stradlater in the bathroom while the other boy shaves. We can see from his description that Holden both dislikes Stradlater for his egotism and true nature, but also recognizes that other people find him attractive.

Stradlater is getting ready for a date and asks Holden to do his homework for him: writing a short essay. Holden hints that he might do it. He fools around while Stradlater shaves, dancing and role-playing like he's in a movie. Then he starts wrestling with Stradlater, annoying his roommate as he tries to look sharp for his date. Holden asks who the date is with and Stradlater says that she knows Holden and that her name is Jean Gallagher. Holden is shocked and corrects Stradlater – her name is actually *Jane* Gallagher.

Holden knows Jane from last summer when they were neighbors and played checkers together. He reminisces and clearly has fond memories and is attracted to Jane. He also resents that Stradlater seems to not even know her name and is only looking to have sex with her.

Holden lends Stradlater the jacket he'd asked for. We see that Stradlater is more popular than Holden and knows how to manipulate people into doing what he wants. However, Holden recognizes a lot of this and is more immune, being his roommate.

Holden is nervous about a nice girl like Jane going out with a conceited jerk like Stradlater, worried that she might go too far with him. Holden tends to divide people into two groups – the pure and the impure, and he doesn't like the idea of Jane (pure) associating with Stradlater (impure). Jane has only signed out of her dorm until 9:30 p.m., so it's possible Stradlater may not get very far with her.

Once Stradlater has left, Holden worries to himself for half an hour until Ackley shows up again. Holden is almost glad to have him around to get his mind off Stradlater and Jane.

CHAPTER 5: Holden eats a lackluster meal in the cafeteria and then goes outside to throw snowballs with a few other boys. He decides with his friend Mal Brossard to take a bus to downtown Agerstown to see a movie, and Holden wants to ask Ackley to come along. Brossard and Ackley don't really like each other, but they both agree to go along. Holden tries to take a snowball onto the bus but the driver won't let him.

Holden's friends have both seen the movie at the theater so they just eat and fool around before heading back to Pencey. They kill more time there doing nothing until Holden is alone and writes Stradlater's English homework. The homework is to write a descriptive passage, so Holden writes about a baseball mitt that belonged to his dead brother Allie. This passage really allows us to know a little more about Holden and can be seen as a clever *exposition* (the author's way of informing the reader about the past). We learn that Allie was two years younger than Holden and he died when he was only 11 (Holden was 13 at the time). When Allie died of leukemia,

Holden broke all the windows in the garage with his fist. We can see that when Holden cares about people, when he admits them past his many defenses, he keeps them very close to his heart.

CHAPTER 6: When Holden's roommate Stradlater arrives home from his date, Holden is naturally curious to find out what happened between him and Jane. Stradlater looks at the composition Holden wrote, sees that it's about a baseball glove and gets angry. He wants a description of a room or a house — something like that, not a glove. Annoyed with Stradlater, Holden rips up the composition, which angers Stradlater even more.

They talk about Stradlater's date. Stradlater borrowed the basketball coach's car (because he's an important member of the team) and Holden wants to know what happened in the car. He's afraid Stradlater may have had sex with Jane. As they talk, Stradlater lightly punches or shadow boxes Holden's shoulder. Along with the Jane Gallagher situation, it frustrates Holden and he tries to punch Stradlater, hardly even hitting him. Stradlater fights back and subdues Holden, who repeatedly calls Stradlater a moron and loses his cool. Stradlater finally lets him up and tells him to shut up, but Holden berates him again and Stradlater punches him and bloodies his face. He then stops and tells Holden to get his face cleaned up. After all that, Holden continues to insult Stradlater.

When Holden sees himself in the mirror, he looks horrible. He's fascinated by the damage done to his face. Curious if Ackley had heard all the noise from the fight, Holden peaks his head into his neighbor's room. He says he does so to see what Ackley is doing and that he doesn't usually go in that room. But it seems more likely that he wants to be away from Stradlater and get some sympathy from Ackley, who also dislikes Stradlater.

CHAPTER 7: Holden goes into Ackley's room and starts asking him questions. Ackley is annoyed and just wants to sleep. He is Catholic and has Mass in the morning.

Holden tells Ackley about the fight with Stradlater and wants to sleep in the empty bed in Ackley's room. It belongs to Ely, Ackley's roommate, who is gone for the weekend. But Ackley doesn't want to let Holden sleep in his roommate's bed. He doesn't want Ely to come in and find Holden there. But Holden lies down anyway and Ackley soon falls asleep. Holden can't however, because he's still worried about Stradlater and Jane Gallagher.

He knows Stradlater's technique with women and thinks he's actually slept with girls, that he's not just talk.

He hears Stradlater using the bathroom and wakes up Ackley, who is again annoyed. Holden asks him about joining a monastery. Ackley thinks Holden is mocking his religion so Holden steps out into the hall. It's very quiet and Holden is antsy. He decides that he won't wait till Wednesday to leave Pencey. He'll leave *now* and stay in a cheap hotel in New York with the money his grandmother sent him.

He wakes a boy down the hall who had borrowed his typewriter and sells it to him. Then he packs and feels depressed when he sees the ice skates his mother sent him. As he leaves, he shouts, "Sleep tight, ya morons!"

We see further evidence in this chapter that Holden is very impulsive, making snap decisions based on how he feels in the given moment.

CHAPTER 8: Holden walks to the train station in the snow and is very cold. He can't take a taxi because it's so late. He gets to the station and a train quickly arrives. He usually likes riding trains, but not tonight. The whole situation has made him uneasy.

When the train stops in Trenton, New

Jersey, a woman in her 40s gets on and sits right next to Holden, even though the train is empty. She's carrying a large bag and wants to sit near the front. Holden finds her attractive despite the age difference and strikes up a conversation with her. It turns out her son goes to Pencey as well. Holden knows him – his name is Ernest Morrow – and he doesn't like him.

Holden begins to tell all kinds of lies. He lies about how all the boys admire Ernest at school. He lies about his name. He starts to feel a little bad about the lies because the woman is so nice, but he finds he can't stop. He even lies about the reason he's leaving: he says he is going to have an operation to remove a brain tumor.

He smokes and gives her a cigarette as well, then invites her to join him for a drink in the club car. She declines and gets off at Newark, New Jersey, and invites Holden to visit them in Massachusetts. But Holden dislikes her son and thinks, "But I wouldn't visit that sonuvabitch Morrow for all the dough in the dough in the world, even if I was desperate."

The persona that Holden put on in this chapter is just one of the many faces he'll wear as he interacts with people in the book. Where is the real Holden under these masks?

We'll have to wait quite a while before we see that.

CHAPTER 9: Holden arrives at Penn Station in New York and wants to call someone. He considers calling his younger sister Phoebe but knows she's already asleep. He thinks about Jane Gallagher and another girl he knows named Sally Hayes, but doesn't call either. Finally he just gets a taxi. He gives the driver his home address till he remembers his plan to stay at a cheap hotel. He asks the driver to turn around, and then mentions something he's been wondering about since he went to see his teacher Mr. Spencer: he wants to know what happens to the ducks on the pond in Central Park when the water freezes over in the winter – where do they go? He asks the driver and the man looks at Holden like he's crazy.

Holden gets to the Edmont hotel and checks in. It's a cheap hotel and a cheap room. Holden looks out the window and sees "perverts" (as he puts it) in neighboring rooms. One man is putting on women's clothing. He also sees a couple squirting liquid back and forth from each other's mouths. Holden is both fascinated and disgusted.

He is still feels anxious and wants to do something, call somebody. He says that he's horny. Then he remembers a phone number a guy gave him for a girl in New York named Faith Cavendish who has a reputation for being loose. Holden phones her. She's initially annoyed that he's calling so early, but she warms up to him when it sounds like he might have money. He wants to meet her right away but she wants to wait till the next day. They reach an impasse and Holden regrets telling her that he can only meet her now.

CHAPTER 10: Holden still can't sleep. It's very early in the morning and he still wants to talk to people. He thinks about his sister Phoebe again and it's clear she's one of the closest people to him, despite her young age (10). She's very intelligent and has a good understanding of Holden.

Instead of calling her, Holden goes to the hotel club called the Lavender Room. It's a dive. He dislikes the band and the place is nearly empty. The waiter won't let him order alcohol. He notices some women at a nearby table and one of them catches his eye. They are tourists from Seattle, Washington. He begins talking with them and asks them to dance. He dances with the blond one who initially attracted him.

She's a good dancer but a poor conversationalist, obsessed with movie stars

and things Holden despises. She dislikes it
when he uses strong language. He tries to
compliment her and kiss her forehead but she
gets angry at him. After dancing, they sit
down and Holden finds them all stupid. He
can't have a real conversation and gets sore at
them when they ask his age. Then they get up
and leave and Holden pays their bill, a little
miffed that they didn't even offer to pay for
the drinks they had before he arrived. Holden
leaves as the Lavender Room is closing, still
sore that he couldn't get any alcohol.

CHAPTER 11: In the hotel lobby Holden
spends most of this chapter remembering his
friend Jane Gallagher, who he still can't get
off his mind. They never got too physical, but
he still felt very close to her.

He recalls how they met. Her dog used to
crap on Holden's lawn and this irritated his
mother. When Holden saw Jane near the pool
he struck up a conversation with her and they
became friends. They played golf and
checkers together.

One day while playing checkers, Jane's
stepfather (who both she and Holden
disliked) asked Jane where his cigarettes were.
She wouldn't answer him, and then she
wouldn't speak to Holden and a tear fell from
her eye. Holden began to kiss her all over her

face. He asked her if the guy had ever tried to touch Jane sexually, and she said no, and Holden never did find out what exactly was the matter.

Holden thinks about all this in the lobby and about Stradlater trying to get with her. Still anxious and uneasy, Holden takes a cab to Ernie's, a night club in Greenwich Village that Holden used to go to with his brother D.B. Ernie is a great piano player, although conceited.

CHAPTER 12: In the taxi ride to Ernie's, Holden again asks the driver about the ducks in the lagoon in Central Park. "Do you happen to know where they go in the wintertime, by any chance?"

This driver also thinks that Holden is nutty for even asking and it seems to really rile him. They discuss where the fish go also, since they obviously can't leave. They come to the conclusion that the fish live in the frozen ice, absorbing nutrition through it. This is definitely not true – in reality, only the upper layer of water turns to ice, the lower layers remain as water and the fish live in it.

Holden gets to Ernie's and the place is packed with college students and Holden can't stand how everyone is treating Ernie like his playing is holy. Holden says the only reason he's there is so he won't have to be alone. He is annoyed by the people he sees and hears. Then a girl named Lillian Simmons recognizes him. She used to date D.B., Holden's brother. She's with a Navy guy who Holden thinks is uptight. She invites Holden to join them and he says he was just leaving. He didn't want to leave, but he must if he's to avoid joining them. He and the Navy guy say it was nice to meet each other, but it's obvious neither means it. Holden is clearly being a *phony*, what he hates most in others, but he justifies it: "If you want to stay alive, you have to say that stuff, though."

CHAPTER 13: Rather than taking another taxi and a driver he dislikes, Holden walks the 41 blocks back to his hotel. His hands are cold and he wishes he'd been able to find his gloves when he was packing. He thinks someone stole them, but even if he knew who'd done it he probably wouldn't have had the nerve to confront the guy. He says that he's a bit of a coward when it comes to fistfights. He especially can't stand to see somebody get punched in the face.

He feels lousy and wants to stop and have another drink, but instead he just gives a guy who comes out of a bar directions.

He gets back to the hotel and takes the

elevator up to his room. The guy operating the elevator is named Maurice and he asks Holden if he wants a prostitute. Maurice says it's five dollars for a short time, and fifteen dollars to have the girl till noon. Holden unthinkingly says he'll just take a "throw" — that is, a short time. Maurice says he'll send a girl to his room.

While Holden waits for her, he gets spruced up. Even if she is just a prostitute, he wants to look okay. He admits to us at this time that he's still a virgin, although he says there have been many times when he could have lost his virginity.

When the girl arrives, Holden thinks she's kind of young and loses his nerve. Her name is Sunny. She takes off her dress and that makes him more uncomfortable. He wants to just talk to her and she gets rude. She wants to know why Holden sent for her if he didn't want sex. He tells a lie about a recent operation. Sunny says he'll still have to pay and that it's ten dollars. Holden says the price agreed upon was five, not ten, and refuses to give her more than five.

She leaves and Holden finds the whole experience stressful.

CHAPTER 14: Holden sits and smokes for a good while after Sunny is gone. He imagines talking to his dead brother Allie, something he does when he's depressed. He finally gets in bed and thinks about praying, but he's an atheist and it won't mean anything to him. He explains how he likes Jesus but not other people in the Bible, like the Disciples.

Then there's a knock at the door and he has a bad feeling he knows who it is. He opens it and Maurice and Sunny are there. They come into his room and say he owes them five more dollars. He tells them they're crooks and Maurice said it would only be five dollars. It looks like Maurice might rough Holden up to get the money, but then Sunny finds Holden's wallet and just takes it. They're about to leave when Holden calls Maurice a "dirty moron" and tells him he'll be begging in the street in a few years. Maurice hits Holden in the stomach and they leave.

Holden staggers to the bathroom pretending he's been shot in the gut. He then has a fantasy about shooting Maurice with a gun and then having Jane Gallagher come over to bandage Holden up. Realizing the ludicrous nature of his fantasy, he says, "The goddam movies. They can ruin you. I'm not kidding."

He takes a bath and goes back to bed, saying that he'd commit suicide if he only thought they would cover him up after he landed on the pavement. He wouldn't want people to be staring at him as a bloody mess.

CHAPTER 15: Holden wakes up around ten that Sunday morning. He's hungry, but doesn't want to order room service because they might send up Maurice. He calls Sally Hayes and makes a date with her to see a matinee show.

He decides to check out of the hotel. He takes his suitcase to Grand Central Station and puts it in a storage locker. Then he goes to a diner and eats a big breakfast. He thinks about cheap luggage, and how it can make him hate a person.

While eating he talks with some nuns who he likes. He discusses English literature with one of them, explaining why he didn't like some parts of *Romeo and Juliet*. Even though he is low on money, he makes a ten dollar donation to the nuns (he also tries to pay their bill, but they refuse). He is very glad they don't ask him if he is Catholic – he's known people who do that and he really hates it. Then he accidentally blows smoke in their faces and he feels guilty about it and apologizes profusely. He wishes he had given them more money, and thinks, "Goddam money. It always ends up making you blue as hell."

CHAPTER 16: After breakfast, Holden walks toward Broadway. He considers how none of the women he knows would ever do something like collect money in an old straw basket. He's also saddened that those nuns will never have a fancy lunch in a nice restaurant.

As he walks, he hears a kid singing "Comin' Thro' the Rye," the Robert Burns poem, but Holden misremembers and thinks the line is, "If a body *catch* a body coming through the rye," replacing *meet* with *catch*.

Holden sees a lot of people waiting in line for movies and he's sickened by it. He goes to a record store to buy a copy of "Little Shirley Beans," a record he heard at Pencey. He's getting it for his sister Phoebe.

Bored, he almost calls Jane Gallagher again. Instead, he gets tickets to a Broadway show. He hates movies and actors in general, but thinks live shows are better than movies. He gets tickets to a show called *I Know My Love* that features a famous husband-wife acting team known as "the Lunts."

Eager to get off Broadway, he takes a cab to Central Park and hopes he'll see Phoebe. She's not there, but he talks with a little girl who knows her and suggests that Holden check the museum. He points out that it's Sunday, so that can't be the case. Holden helps the girl tighten her skate, and then walks to the museum anyway. He reminisces about his own trips to the museum in elementary school and how it was always different, even though the museum stayed the same, *he* changed. When he gets to the museum, he changes his mind about entering. He gets another taxi and goes to the Biltmore hotel, where he agreed to meet Sally Hayes for their date.

CHAPTER 17: Holden waits for Sally Hayes in the lobby of the Biltmore and watches girls. He ruminates on how the girls look (he's clearly horny) and how some people are incredibly boring. Sally arrives. She's delighted he got tickets to the Lunts show. Holden has sarcastic and resentful thoughts about her conversation the entire way, and when they watch the show it's even worse.

At the intermission, Sally recognizes a boy she knows and they talk. Their whole conversation nauseates Holden and his initial affection for Sally begins to sour: "I sort of hated old Sally by the time we got in the cab..."

She suggests they go ice skating at Radio

City. He is hesitant and knows she just wants to show off how cute her butt is in the dress they rent her, but Holden agrees. They skate poorly and Holden is self-conscious from the onlookers. They eventually sit for a drink and Holden unleashes on Sally his whole dissatisfaction with school and life in general. He criticizes New York and the way everyone lives. He suggests that he and Sally go away and live in the woods somewhere. He says he felt like he could actually do it at the time. Sally presents objections and gets on Holden's nerves. His emotions quickly swing (as they've done before) and he suddenly can't stand Sally. He says, "You give me a royal pain in the ass, if you want to know the truth," and this really turns her against him.

They leave separately and he can't understand why he said all he did. He meant how he felt about her at the time, but now he thinks it's crazy. This is the "madman stuff" that he referred to at the beginning of the book – his attempt to break out of the life he's known and into something more authentic. We're beginning to see he has the desire, but not the knowledge and capabilities to do so at this point in his life. Perhaps if he was a few years older or lived in a different decade or century he might attempt a lifestyle similar to Jack Kerouac in *On the Road* or Henry David Thoreau in *Walden*, but in late 1940s New York as a 16-year-old boy, he feels trapped.

CHAPTER 18: As Holden leaves the skating rink he considers calling Jane Gallagher. He called her earlier but her mother answered, so he quickly hung up. He has been longing to see her throughout the book, but he never will. She is part of his elusive longing for something authentic, always out of his grasp. He does call her now, but no one answers. Holden wonders who else he might call. He phones Carl Luce, a boy he knew at another school, and they agree to meet that night for a drink.

In the meantime, Holden goes to the movies at Radio City. He complains about the Christmas show and then he complains about the sappy movie. Complaining about things well within his control is a common pattern for Holden.

The movie makes Holden think about war and how his brother D.B. was in World War II. Holden thinks he would be crazy if he had to be in the army and he can't understand why D.B. recommended Ernest Hemingway's novel *A Farewell to Arms*. He ends the chapter this way: "If there's ever another war, I'm going to sit right the hell on top of it. I'll volunteer for it, I swear to God I will."

CHAPTER 19: Holden begins this chapter talking about the Wicker Bar, how it's a place full of phonies and how he hates it. He's waiting for Luce there and it's pretty crowded. Holden thinks he sees "flits" in the crowd – slang for gay men. He transitions into a description of Luce, who was Holden's student adviser at Whooton, one of his previous schools. He has a sort of admiration for Luce's maturity, sexual experience, and intellectual capabilities. But Holden is also capable of seeing Luce as an uptight snob.

Luce arrives and starts drinking. Holden quizzes him about his sex life and learns he is seeing a Chinese woman in her thirties. Luce is irritated by Holden's immature questions. Holden says he'll stop, but continues with them anyway. He's probably a little drunk at this point. Luce says that Holden needs psychoanalysis – this was very popular in the forties and fifties. Luce's father is an analyst.

Holden wants Luce to stay longer and admits he's lonely, but Luce says he must leave.

CHAPTER 20: Holden remains at the Wicker Bar quite a while longer drinking and waiting for the familiar performers to show up. He gets very drunk and considers calling Jane Gallagher again, but instead calls Sally Hayes and tells her he'll come over to trim the tree on Christmas Eve. She immediately knows he's drunk and soon hangs up on him.

He goes to the restroom and sits on the radiator, complimenting the piano player when he comes in. The man can also see Holden is drunk and encourages him to go home. Holden eventually leaves and walks to the park. He is cold but he wants to see if the ducks are in the pond. On his way, he drops and breaks the record he got for his sister Phoebe. He puts the pieces in his coat pocket. Further evidence that he's extremely drunk comes when he can't even find the pond he's looking for.

He sits on a bench and the cold weather makes him imagine how he'll get pneumonia and die. Alcohol seems to trigger Holden's imagination, and he envisions his relatives all coming from far away for his funeral, as they did when Allie died. He doesn't like the idea of being buried in a cemetery.

As he sits there counting his money, he realizes he only has $4.30 left. He takes four quarters and a nickel and skims them across the ice. This is an example of Salinger "torturing" his character, making him do something he'll regret later.

Holden feels bad when he thinks of Phoebe learning that he's died of pneumonia, so he decides to go home and sneak in to see her. He walks home and is no longer tired or drunk, just cold.

CHAPTER 21: When Holden gets to the building where his family lives, he's pleased to discover there's a new elevator boy who won't recognize Holden and tell the family he was there. Holden wants to sneak in to see his sister and then sneak out. He lies to the elevator boy about visiting his neighbors, then quietly enters his own family's apartment.

It's quiet and dark and he's worried most about his mother hearing him. She has very sensitive hearing. There's a great deal of hyperbolic language in this section. Holden loves to speak in a very exaggerated manner.

He makes his way slowly to his sister's room, but remembers that she always sleeps in D.B.'s room when he's away in Hollywood. So Holden goes to D.B.'s room. He doesn't wake Phoebe right away. He admires the fine clothes his mother has bought her, and looks through her notebook at the cute notes she has made.

When he wakes her, Phoebe is delighted to see him. She talks about the play she is in.

Holden discovers their parents are at a party in Connecticut and won't be home till late. They talk about a boy who seems to have a crush on Phoebe, about the record Holden broke, about D.B. writing a movie about Annapolis, and other things. Phoebe is suspicious that Holden is home early and correctly deduces that he was kicked out of Pencey. Phoebe says, "Daddy's going to kill you," and buries her head in a pillow in sadness. Holden leaves her for a second to get some cigarettes from a box on the living room table.

CHAPTER 22: Holden continues talking with Phoebe, who is still concerned about her father's anger with Holden. He tells her not to worry. The worst that'll happen is Holden will be sent to military school. But he says that won't happen because he'll go away to a ranch in Colorado he says he knows about.

It's ironic that Phoebe seems to be more organized and coherent about the future than Holden. He tries to explain why he couldn't stand Pencey and she says, "You don't like *any*thing that's happening." He says this isn't true, and she tells him to name one thing he likes.

He tries to concentrate and instead thinks of a boy named James Castle at a school he went to. The boy was bullied by other kids until he jumped out a window and killed himself. Holden remembers that the boy had asked to borrow his turtleneck sweater.

When Phoebe prompts him again to name something he likes, he says he likes Allie. He says he likes talking with his sister as they're doing right now. She isn't satisfied with either answer and asks Holden to think of something he wants to be in the future. He refers to the Robert Burns poem (that he heard the boy singing earlier) and says that he'd like to be a catcher in the rye. He misremembers the lyrics and imagines an adult standing at the edge of a cliff as children play in the rye. He would stand at the edge to make sure the children don't fall off the cliff.

Holden then goes to make a phone call in the living room and tells Phoebe not to fall asleep. He will call a former teacher of his, Mr. Antolini.

CHAPTER 23: Mr. Antolini takes Holden's call and tells him he can come over, even though it's very late. Holden tells us that Antolini is a young man. When James Castle killed himself, Antolini covered the boy with his coat and carried him to the infirmary.

After the call, Holden dances with Phoebe and talks some more until they hear a sound.

It's their parents, just returned from the party. Holden puts out his cigarette and hides in the closet. Their mother comes in to say goodnight to Phoebe and smells the smoke. A quick liar like Holden, she tells her mom she tried a cigarette. Her mother doesn't approve. She leaves and Holden comes out. Phoebe wants him to stay there, but he says he'll go to Antolini's. He just needs a little money, which Phoebe gladly lends him. He gives her the red hunting hat he's worn throughout the novel. She wears it to bed.

Holden leaves the house without really caring if he is caught. Foreshadowing the events at Antolini's, he says, "I almost wished they did, in a way."

CHAPTER 24: Holden tells us more about Mr. and Mrs. Antolini. She is quite a bit older than her husband. Mr. Antolini is also acquainted with Holden's family: He has read his brother D.B.'s stories and he had lunch with Holden's father. He asks Holden about why he left Pencey and the boy criticizes a class on Oral Expression that he failed. He liked it when people make digressions in their speech, but there was a very oppressive, judgmental tone to the class that didn't allow that. This relates to the larger issue of Holden's own resistance and dislike of the society as a whole. Mr. Antolini tries to convince Holden that sometimes there are benefits to sticking to one course, in speech or in life. Mr. Antolini has been drinking. Holden just wants to sleep, and is a little peeved that this lecture can't wait till morning.

Mr. Antolini tells Holden he is heading for "a special kind of fall, a horrible kind. The man isn't permitted to feel or hear himself hit bottom. He just keeps falling and falling." Typically, this depresses Holden more.

Mr. Antolini also writes a quote down from the psychoanalyst Wilhelm Stekel: "The mark of the immature man is that he wants to die nobly for a cause, while the mark of the mature man is that he wants to live humbly for one." He wants Holden to apply himself towards some direction in his life, and he stresses the urgency of it.

Holden tries to stifle a yawn but eventually it comes out. Mr. Antolini decides to let him go to sleep on the couch. Holden sleeps a little, then wakes up and discovers Mr. Antolini petting or patting his head. Holden freaks out and can't understand what's going on, and decides Antolini is some kind of pervert. Antolini tells him to keep his voice down. Holden says that he just remembered his bag at the station locker, and that he has to leave. Antolini wants him to wait till morning, but Holden says there is money in the bag he can't leave there. This is of course just an excuse to get out of there right away. Even though he is tired, he is more uncomfortable around Mr. Antolini.

Antolini asks him to come back afterward, and Holden says he will, but it's clear to us he won't. There is an awkward moment in the hall as Holden waits for the elevator and Antolini just watches him and tells him he is "a very, very strange boy."

CHAPTER 25: Holden gets out on the streets of New York in the early hours of the morning. He's tired but doesn't want to spend any more of Phoebe's money to stay in a hotel, so he sleeps on a bench in Grand Central Station. He doesn't sleep well. He's worried that maybe Mr. Antolini wasn't trying to make a sexual pass at him after all. He just isn't sure, and he likes Mr. Antolini for many reasons.

He reads a magazine he finds and it worries him that he has cancer. He walks over to the East Side to find a cheap diner and get breakfast. He orders donuts but finds he can't eat them when they arrive, so he sends them back. He's very depressed. Walking around, he sees a lot of Christmas activities on the streets. He recalls a time when he was crossing the streets and worried that he wouldn't make it to the other side, that he'd just disappear, and he had prayed to his dead brother Allie to let him get across.

Holden lives largely in his imagination this chapter, and he envisions himself hitchhiking west and getting a job at a gas station. He would pretend to be a deaf-mute so he wouldn't have to talk to anyone, and eventually he'd build a cabin in the woods and marry a deaf-mute wife. He really thinks he's going to do it – he just wants to see Phoebe before he leaves to give her back her money.

He goes to her school that morning and writes a note asking her to meet him at the art museum at 12:15 p.m. While he's at the school, he sees the phrase "Fuck you" written on the wall. It really upsets him that kids have to see that. He rubs it off, but later he sees another one and he's unable to rub that off.

From the school, Holden goes to the museum. He has about half an hour to spare so he waits inside. A pair of boys ask him where the mummies are and Holden helps them find them. When he's alone, he sees another "Fuck you" written on the wall and says, "You can't ever find a place that's nice and peaceful, because there isn't any. You may think there is, but once you get there, when you're not looking, somebody'll sneak up and write 'Fuck you' right under your nose."

He's feeling horrible and goes to the bathroom. As he exits the restroom, he passes out, but seems to feel better after that.

He waits for Phoebe some more and worries she won't show and that he'll never see any of his relatives again. He has plans for Phoebe and D.B. to come visit his cabin in the woods. Phoebe does finally show up however.

She has a suitcase with her and says she wants to go with Holden. He tells her no and to shut up. This really gets her mad. To appease her, Holden says he won't leave after all, and that he'll go with Phoebe for a walk to the zoo. She's still angry, but goes along with him.

They go to the carousel in the park after that. Phoebe rides it at Holden's urging and enjoys herself, forgiving Holden in the process. He assures her again that he won't leave to go west.

It starts to rain but Holden doesn't care because he's so happy to see Phoebe riding the carousel and enjoying herself. He concludes the book's action by saying: "It was just that she looked so damn *nice*, the way she kept going around and around, in her blue coat and all. God, I wish you could've been there."

CHAPTER 26: The last chapter is more of an epilogue than anything else. Holden says he doesn't feel like talking about the school he's going to in the fall. He's relating all this from California still, and his brother D.B. has visited him and Holden told him all about the story of those few days.

A psychoanalyst asks Holden if he'll apply himself when he returns to school and Holden is annoyed by the question. He can't say until he actually gets there.

He regrets telling so many people about how he spent those few days. It has made him think about the people more and miss them, even people like Stradlater and Maurice. He concludes: "It's funny. Don't ever tell anybody anything. If you do, you start missing everybody."

CRITICAL QUESTIONS & ESSAY TOPICS

Here are some critical questions and essay topics about the book. These questions may be answered in a variety of ways based on your reading of the text. I have provided suggestions in the answers below, but I encourage you to consider alternative answers as you explore these topics.

1. Why has *The Catcher in the Rye* appealed to so many people?

More than the plot, the attitude and tone of the book have made it appealing to many young people. Holden Caulfield represents an honesty and disillusionment that had not been so explicitly stated before that time, and readers found it unique.

2. Why does Holden go to so many places that he seems to hate?

We witness Holden go to many places (the movies, bars, clubs) that he complains heavily about. Part of this stems from his attitude – he would complain about any place or anything. He continues to go to these places because he feels trapped in his world and sees no other option available to him.

3. Why is Holden so concerned about what happened between Stradlater and Jane Gallagher?

This relates to how Holden views Jane and Stradlater. He views Jane as pure and good, and Stradlater as malicious and selfish. The idea of them meeting together is hard for him to deal with. He cares for Jane in a sentimental way (largely the product of his imagination), and he wants to keep her safe.

4. When Phoebe asks Holden to name something he likes, why does he think of James Castle?

James Castle, the boy who threw himself out a window to escape bullying, represents an innocence that Holden admires in people. He sees it in children and others like James. Holden relates to the feeling of being victimized by a cruel world.

5. Why does Holden want to be a "catcher in the rye"?

The idea of being a nurturing caretaker, of protecting children from the danger of the world, is something that strikes a chord with Holden. But the job or role of "catcher in the rye" is something he perceives as unavailable to him, putting it alongside his other fantasies.

6. How does Holden view children in the novel?

Holden sees an innocence and gentleness in children that he can't find in the adult world. As such, he feels protective and compassionate toward children.

7. Compare and contrast Mr. Spencer and Mr. Antolini.

Holden cannot connect to Mr. Spencer when he goes to meet him. He feels the old man is talking *to* him rather than *with* him. Mr. Antolini, on the other hand, is someone Holden can relate to, but because of the strange action (petting or patting Holden's head) when he awakes, Holden feels betrayed by Mr. Antolini.

8. How are Holden's parents depicted in the story?

Holden never directly interacts with his

parents in the novel. Based on his mother's conversation with Phoebe and other hints, they seem like caring people. They are probably nicer than Holden likes to imagine. They put up with his many failures at school, and have sent him to a rest home out west (rather than immediately sending him to military school, for instance). They seem to have sympathy for Holden, and are trying to understand the psychological issues going on within him.

9. What is Holden trying to accomplish over the course of his few days in the city? Or is he simply killing time until he goes home?

Underneath his seemingly random actions, Holden is trying to make a genuine connection with people. He doesn't seem ready to admit this to himself, and he settles for many inferior alternatives along the way.

10. How does Holden reconcile his hatred of "phonies" with his own lies?

Holden puts on many masks throughout the book, usually trying to appear older and more mature than he is. Because he knows he is being phony when he does this, he carries an underlying self-loathing and low self-esteem.

11. Is Holden changed by the events of the novel in a significant way?

This is a difficult question to answer. Yes, he does abandon his plan to go west, accede to his sister's wishes, and reach some kind of resolution with his parents. However, it's hard to say if he's genuinely *changed*. He is still very bitter and largely uncaring about his future. All we see at the book's conclusion is that he'll sustain himself a little longer. That might lead to change, but it's too soon to say now.

CONCLUSION

The Catcher in the Rye is a modern classic, as popular today as when it was first released. It unsettles us and asks difficult questions about how we live. I hope this guide has helped you navigate this book, and deepened your understanding of all that occurs in its pages.